TABLE OF CONTENT

Brief Contents

Dedication

This book is dedicated to all aspirational millionaires who intend to make money

This book is dedicated to all aspirational millionaires who intend to

PREFACE

Does investing look complex or overwhelming to you? This guide to investing cuts through the many steps and explains what you really need to know. This simple and straightforward book for beginners will have you investing like a professional. When it comes to understanding how to invest, the biggest challenge can be figuring out where to commence. Finances can be deterred in their complexity, but investing shouldn't be complex and intimidating. Simple investing strategies are better to deal with. If you are ready to start investing and are looking for a simple guide, this book will help you get your financial life together.

Book Description

The five simple guides to investing offer a brief, non-technical introduction to investing, and the implementation and management of investments. It is directed toward investors who wish to understand critical asset management problems without even having to become experts in the fields of finance and economics.

However, in the field of managing assets, it is very rare to find uniformity of opinion. Several investors usually find it challenging to understand heterogeneous viewpoints. This book does not evangelize for any school of thought nor does it avoid pointing out controversies in academic research.

This book provides the reader with the findings and conclusions of intentional individuals who employ differing opinions along a spectrum of academic approaches. The sole aim of this book is to provide investors with information substantial to enable them to work efficiently. This book gives the basics and the implications of investment choices. The truth is, investing sounds easy but it is not. Investors in today's financial markets face many challenges when deciding how to invest their money.

This book is specially designed to help beginners understand the reasons to invest and also those of asset classes and also equip them with the tools needed to answer the basic questions

that will help shape their investment
strategy.

CHAPTER 1

Introduction to Investing

I'm sure we've all heard the saying 'investing for the future'. But what does this really mean? How does investing work, and why is it very important? Investing is quite different from saving or trading. Your savings can be insured but investments are not. Investing is a strategy to set aside money while you are occupied with life and have that money you invested work for you so that you can reap the rewards of your investment in future.

Investing simply put is when you use your finances to purchase assets which you hope will increase in value in the long run. These assets could be real assets such as a house or gold. Or they could be a financial asset such as shares in companies or bonds issued by the government or by companies. The aim of investment is to put money to work in one or more types of investment plans in the hopes of growing your money over time.

Investing saves money for the future hoping that it will grow with time. Investing is all about setting yourself up for a long-term financial success in future. The downside of this is that investing comes with a lot of risks. Investing can be a complex prospect for beginners with an enormous variety of likely assets to add to a portfolio. The investment risk ladder recognizes asset classes based on their relative riskiness. Cash is the most stable and alternative investment often being the most unstable.

Today, investing in the stock market is the most common and preferable way for beginners to gain investment experience. Investing is all about risks. The returns you get are linked to the perceived level of risk involved. In investing, you make good use of higher rates of return and benefiting from the power of compound interest over long periods of time, it's all about finding the best ways to manage the risks involved. In the world today, investing is gradually changing terrain, especially as technology is evolving. Investment work on the basis that any selected investment brings monetary returns. The main purpose of investing is to create returns. The returns created may be a gain or a loss, depreciation, investment income or a combination of both capital gain and income. The return can include currency gains or losses due to the diverse foreign currency exchange rates. Investors expect higher returns from a risky investment. When a less risky investment is made, the return is low.

The most common investment terms are instability and returns. These terms are two sides of a coin. The more unstable or volatile an investment is, the more returns you would expect in the long run. A higher volatility often comes with an increased risk factors. Before investing, investors need to take into consideration several factors when deciding if the investment has growth potential. You need to look at the historical returns, risk factors, competitors and also calculations. This will help you decide if it's right for you or not. Most investors invest to get a higher return on their assets than what they will get from just saving the same amount of money.

Since there is inflation, investors want to receive returns way higher than what they would be keeping in the bank. This implies that you must grow the money you already have.

CHAPTER 2

Reasons   to   Invest

Why do people invest? It's fine if you have different answers to this question but it will be an issue if you don't. When investing, you need to be very alert. Having clear reasons before investing is very crucial to investing successfully. Before investing, it is important to set a goal so you know why you are investing your money. Investing allows your money to grow irrespective of inflation and increase in value. Below are some reasons people invest:

➢ To reach financial goals:

Investing in assets can help you reach big financial goals. It has been established that the more volatile, the higher the returns. If your investment is earning a higher rate of return than a savings account, you will be earning money both over the long term and also within a fast period. This return you get can be used towards a major financial goal, such as purchasing a new car, buying a home or even starting your own business and paying for tuition for your children.

➢ To grow your money:

The main aim of investing is simply to grow your money. Investing your money can assist you to grow it. Certain investment vehicles such as bonds, stocks, and deposits, offer returns on your money in the long run. These returns allow your money to grow thus creating wealth over time. The value of a company grows over time as the amount of profit it makes increases. This growth will be reflected in the price of the company's shares also.

➢ To support others:

Some investors prefer to invest in people, they could be business owners, artists or even manufacturers. When they invest they feel good helping others achieve their goals over time.

➢ To save for retirement:

As you earn, it is important to also save money for retirement. You can comfortably put your savings into a portfolio of investments, such as stocks, real estate, bonds, mutual funds, precious metals such as gold, and businesses. When you eventually retire, you can live off the funds you've earned from these investments. You need to be more conservative with your investments as you get older, especially as you near retirement age.

➢ To earn higher returns:

To grow your money, you need to invest in a place where you can earn a high rate of return. The higher the return rate, the more money you earn. Investment plans offer the opportunity to earn higher rates than savings accounts.

➢ To reduce the effects of inflation:

Inflation refers to when the prices of goods and services

goes up over time. A slight amount of inflation is a sign of a healthy economy. Too much inflation is very bad for the economy, especially when expectations of higher inflation lead to demands for higher wages which in turn creates greater demand for goods and services. Investing is one way you can protect your savings from the effects of inflation especially if the value of your investment increases at a higher rate than the inflation. Investing in shares offers a bigger chance of beating inflation over a longer term compared to cash and bonds.

➢ To start and expand a business: Investing is an important aspect of business creation and expansion. Most investors support entrepreneurs and contribute to the creation of new jobs and new products. They help create and establish new businesses that can help them with a good return on investment.

➢ To reduce taxable income:

Investors invest in pre-tax dollars into a retirement fund to reduce taxable income.

➢ To protect your purchasing power:

One of the many benefits of investing rather than leaving your money in your savings account is the opportunity to protect your purchasing power during an inflation surge. A country's inflation rate can greatly affect investment.

- ➢ To earn more than just saving in your savings account

  Just putting your money in a savings account may seem like the best way to safeguard your financial future. Investing that money offers you the opportunity to beat inflation and also provide a greater percentage return than you would receive from a savings account. It gives you the chance to take charge of your finances rather than to rely on the decisions of the government.

- ➢ Diversify your income.

  Investing gives you access to multiple streams of income. The benefits of multiple streams of income cannot be overemphasized.

- ➢ It helps you to support causes that are important to you.

If you are interested in supporting a cause such as ending poverty, you can support it by investing in related companies and brands that are trying to make a positive difference. Some shares comes with voting rights, so aside your financial investment, you can also play a part in shaping the direction of any company of your choice.

➢ To gain knowledge

If you choose to succeed in investing, you have a lot of learning to do. It is considered that investing is a venture that is suitable for minds that are enthusiastic to learn and that seek stimulation.

CHAPTER 3

Types of Investment

There are numerous types of investments that serve as tools to help you achieve your financial goals. Each of these investment types has its own set of features, risk factors and ways in which they can be used by investors. They include:

✓ Bonds:

A bond is defined as a loan an investor makes to a company, government or other organizations in exchange for interest payments over a specified term plus repayment of principal at the agreed bond maturity date. There are several types of bonds. They include treasuries, corporate bonds, agency bonds, municipal bonds and many more. When you invest in bonds, you face the risk of losing money, especially if you bought an individual bond and need to sell it before it matures. Bonds and bond mutual can be a very important component of your portfolio.

✓ Mutual funds:

Funds come in different types, they could be mutual funds, unit investment, closed end funds, exchange traded funds. They should be registered as securities and exchange commissions in investment companies. Funds can offer diversification management, they feature a wide variety of investment methods. Investing a fund also comes with its risks, including the possibility that you may lose money.

✓ Options:

These are contracts that give the buyer the right, but not the obligation to buy or sell a security, such as a stock or exchange traded fund at a fixed amount within a specific period of time. This helps investors manage risks, although there are still risks involved, it is possible to lose money. It is important to learn about different types of options, trading strategies and also the risks involved.

✓ Annuities:

This is a contract between you and an insurance company whereby the company promises to make periodic payments to you which can start immediately or in as time goes on. You can buy an annuity either with a single payment or a series of payments called premiums. The common types of annuities are fixed and variable.

✓ Stocks:

This is also known as shares or equities, it is the most common type of investment. It allows investors to partake in the company's success via increases in the stock price and dividends. Companies sell shares of stock to raise cash. On the other hand, investors can then purchase and also sell the stocks among themselves.

✓ Real Estate:

Interested investors can acquire real estate by simply purchasing commercial or residential properties. Investors can equally obtain shares in real estate investment trusts. This acts like mutual funds whereby a group of investors pool their money together to purchase properties.

✓ Exchange traded fund:

This is a type of index fund. They are passively managed funds which invest pooled funds in diversified securities. Here, they track a benchmark index and aim to mirror that index performance. Investors buy into a collection of assets that are purchased and traded in shares.

✓ Commodities:

These could be metals, oil, grain, or animal products. Investing in commodities poses a high risk and they tend not to deliver as much growth as securities either.

✓ Cryptocurrency:

This is a new investment option with bitcoin being the most famous cryptocurrency.

Cryptocurrencies are digital currencies not substantiated by the government or any company. These digital assets are created by companies or individuals that take the form of a virtual coin or token.

✓ Equity:

You invest in equity when you buy shares of stock in an individual corporation or shares in a mutual fund or exchange traded fund.

Other important types of investments worthy of mention are:

✓ Index fund

✓ Share

✓ Hedge fund

✓ Money market fund

✓ Fixed deposits

✓ Corporate bond

✓ Certificate of deposits

✓ Derivative

✓ Preferred Stock

✓ Municipal bond.

What are Alternative Investments? Alternative investments are investments that do not belong to the traditional asset classes of stocks, cash and bonds. Alternative investments include commodities, real estate, hedge funds, cryptocurrencies and many more. These however offer portfolio diversification, can be more complex, riskier and less transparent than traditional investments.

CHAPTER 4

Questions to ask before investing

Before you make an investment, whether it is in a business opportunity, an individual or a marketing program, there are many aspects of it you should consider. The following are some questions you should be able to answer.

1) What is my goal in investment?

This is one of many questions you should ask yourself. What are you trying to accomplish? Your investment plan will differ vastly if, for example, you are trying to save money for your retirement versus trying to save money for a down payment on a car. You need to ask yourself if the investment plan is likely to assist you to achieve your goal.

2) Should I be the sole manager of my investments?

It is tough for a typical investor to beat a highly paid full-time investment professional. If you are always busy and don't have the time or inclination to manage your investment, you should consider hiring a professional to do that for you.

3) What happens if you make losses?

There is a possibility that an investment you made could go to zero. You need to ask yourself if you will be financially devastated if this happens, and also what plans you'll need to put in place if it happens. If your answer is yes, you should not make the investment.

4) Why do you still own that investment?

It is important to regularly go through your investment portfolio to decide if you still want to own your investment. Selling an investment because of a loss is very difficult. Professional investors don't have any emotional entanglement with their investments. They can easily diversify themselves of an investment without working themselves as the investment continues to grow.

5) What is your investment time frame?

The longer your investment time frame, the more risk you can accept in your portfolio because you will now have more time to recover from a mistake. For example, if you are saving for retirement and you are years away from retiring, investing in something illiquid will be meaningful. But if you need the money sooner, you should make investments in something liquid. You need to examine the startups' track record. It makes it easier to know how long the investment horizon will be.

6) Do you have special knowledge of what you are investing in?

Ordinary people have a huge advantage over investment professionals in the fields where they work because an investment professional will never know more about an industry than someone who actually works in it. As a beginner, you should avoid investing in something you don't understand. Always remember to read an investment prospectus statement carefully before investing.

7) Who am I investing with?

It is challenging to judge the character and abilities of anyone based on what you have seen in a company's annual report. It is important to know with whom you are trusting with your money. Things you need to look out for are long, successful records and compensation schemes that reward such investors.

8) When and why will you sell your investment?

If you understand why you are investing, you should also have an idea of when you are going to sell it. If you bought a stock because you were to receive a 20 per cent revenue growth per year, you should plan on selling the stock if the revenue growth does not meet your expectations. If you purchased a stock because you were convenient with the dividend yield, sell the stock if the dividend yield drops.

9) Is the investment registered? Registration is very necessary because it provides investors with the access to key information about the company's management, products, services and finances. Smart investors will always check whether an investment is registered before venturing into it.

10) Does the risks compare with the potential rewards?

The greater the risks involved, the greater the returns. Investments with a higher risk may offer higher potential returns, but they may expose you to greater investment losses. Always remember that every investment offers the best of both worlds. Some investment frauds are pitched as high return opportunities with little or no risk.

The bottom line is that investing in startups is a good opportunity for investors to expand their portfolios and contribute to an entrepreneur's success. Sometimes, a company may have strong cash flow projections, but what looks pleasant on paper may not translate to the real world.

Required steps to know you are ready to invest. Below are some highlights of the things you need to check to know if you are ready to start investing:

Step 1

Know your Goals:

You should not enter investment with only a vague knowledge of it. Set goals to know what you want in the long run.

Step 2

Do you have savings?

It is very important to have some sort of financial buffer in case anything happens along the line.

Step 3

Make sure you have no debt.

Step 4

Make sure you have a responsible attitude to growing your wealth.

Step 5

You should have the motivation to learn.

CHAPTER 5

Simple guide to investing

If you want to become an investor, there are certain step-by-step guides to get started with. Investment is for anyone, regardless of their age. Investing can seem intimidating but the best thing you can do is just to start. Investing gives your money value. When you invest, your money can keep up with inflation and it can help you get on track for financial independence.

Investing is one of the ways to achieve many monetary goals. Sometimes, it's easier to just put off investing for another time, especially when there are bills to pay and other financial responsibilities start to pile up. However, the sooner you start, the more you will have in the long run also, and the more compound interest can work in your favour. You need to do your homework before getting started. You don't necessarily have to learn the intricate ways of the market before you start investing. There are several platforms that can handle that for you. Before you invest, these basic and simple steps can get you on the right track, these steps include:

★ Set a budget

Before investing, you need to decide on how much you will put towards your investment. This can help you decide other parts of your investment strategy like how much you can contribute regularly, where to open your account and also the securities you invest in. The first step and most important aspect in achieving your financial goals are to thoroughly understand your expenses. It is also important to know what you are trying to attain. It doesn't count if you decide to start out small. Even if you have other financial responsibilities, there are ways you can still invest.

It is important you pay off large debts before investing, this doesn't stop you from investing. Normally, you have a huge chunk of money to invest, but most people prefer a slow and steady approach. You should decide how much you plan to invest per week or per month and then plan to set that aside. You should keep in mind that when you invest money, you're putting it at risk. This simply means that you could get back less than you invest. There is a potential that your money could grow too, of course, that's why people do it but there is also the risk that you could lose money also. It is important that you keep an emergency fund. This will give you peace of mind that you would have money available without needing to dip into your investment fund.

★   Know the kind of investor you are.

To figure out the type of investor you are, you need to take into consideration the risk tolerance, how much do you intend to spend in managing your account, and when do you plan to make use of the money. If you are more of a set it and forget it kind of person, you need to invest in funds that give you exposure to multiple holdings instead of buying individual stocks, bonds or other assets you can monitor more closely. Target date funds are suitable for the set it and forget it approach. These funds automatically adjust your risk tolerance based on your age. Just because this method means it will adjust itself doesn't mean you should stop checking in on your investments and continue to invest money regularly.

★ Look for the right platform.

The type of investor you want to be will determine the platform you make use of. If you are new to investing, robo advisors can be a great option for you. These are software run platforms that ask you questions about your risk tolerance and investment time to choose the best investments for you. Some investments come without risks, but the ones with the greatest risk stand to bring the greatest gains but also the greatest losses. You need to understand that your returns will rise and fall over the years. Investing is considered a long term and not a short term activity. It is not a smart strategy to sell your investments for less than you paid for them.

★ You should open an account and invest

At this stage, it is time to open your account, deposit cash and choose your investment type. Do not bother too much about your opening deposit since you can always add funds regularly to your account. As a beginner, you can start with any amount of money as you would like. After opening your account, you should keep it simple. You can start with index mutual funds which can track a specific stock index. As a beginner, that should serve your needs.

★ Keep checking on your investment.

It is important to always check on your investment portfolio regularly. Fix time to review your investments once in a month or even every quarter. The platform should be able to automate your investment. The easiest way to ensure you add to your investment account is to automate regular contributions. You can achieve that by payroll deduction, online banking or the company's website. The longer you leave your money invested, the more time it grows and recover from setbacks.

Things to deliberate on before making an investment decision:

- Take your time to draw a personal financial roadmap: The

first step to investing successfully is to figure out your goals and risk involved. There is zero guarantee that you will make money from your investment. If you plan properly, you should be able to do well.

- Understand the risks involved before investing: There is a reward for taking on risks. It brings higher returns.

- Choose an appropriate mix of investments: As an investor, if you include asset categories with investment returns that fluctuate under different market conditions within a portfolio, you can comfortably protect against significant losses.

- Be careful if you are investing heavily into the shares of an employer's stock or any individual stock: It is very important you diversify your investment. Do not have a single plan, be versatile. If you pick the right group of investments within an asset category, you may be able to limit your losses and also reduce the fluctuations of investment returns without sacrificing much.

- Create a financial buffer: As an investor, you should have an emergency fund. You can put an amount of money in a savings product to cover an emergency.

- Pay off credit card debt: If you owe money on high interest credit cards, the best thing to do is to pay off the balance as quickly as possible.

- You should assess dollar cost averaging: With this, you can protect yourself from the risk of investing all your money at the wrong time by following a consistent pattern of adding money to your investment.

- Make good use of free money from an employer.

- Reexamine your portfolio regularly: You should rebalance your portfolio occasionally. This is simply bringing your portfolio back to your original asset allocation mix. By doing so, you will return your portfolio to a certain level of risk. You can decide to balance your portfolio based on the calendar or on your investments. It is highly recommended that you balance your portfolio. You should do that when the relative weight of an asset class increases or decreases more than a particular percentage. Rebalancing works best when it is done on a relatively infrequent basis.

- Avoid situations that can lead to fraud: It is very important for you to properly investigate and ask solid questions about any investment you wish to start. You should speak with trusted friends and family members. They should be able to guide you before you take any decision. Avoid indulging in activities that can jeopardise your investment. You should meet the right people, ask the right questions. Do the right thing and not deviate from it.

Below are five takeaway tips on how to start investing:

1) You should save up an emergency fund of 3 to 6 months worth of living costs before you invest.

2) You should be prepared not to touch your investment for at least 5 years.

3) You should think about starting small and setting up regular contributions.

4) You can use your ISA allowance when you invest in order to protect more of your money from tax.

5) You should consider taking advice to help you decide what's right for you.

CHAPTER 6

How to invest rightly and   beat inflation

For you to invest rightly during inflation, it is required of you to look for the best investments. Inflation has become an unavoidable fact of life in every economy today. The current economic conditions have created uncertainty for investors and their portfolios. Inflation is rising every day and the government tries to keep it under control.

During inflation, experts recommend you invest in the following:

- TIPS
- Cash
- Short term bonds

- Stocks

- Real estate

- Gold

- Commodities

- Cryptocurrency

Many investors have been used to decades of stable financial conditions and may be wondering what moves to make in order to protect their investments. We hear about inflation every day and we think about how inflation is impacting our investments. Inflation is the silent wealth killer, it has the potential to erode the purchasing power of an investor's portfolio. Below are investment plans investors can use to combat inflation:

1) Investors can beat inflation by investing in gold

Gold is one of the ancient hedge against any economy's inflation. Gold is seen to have an annual gain of 9.48 per cent over the 20 years between September 2001 and September 2021. Within the same period, inflation reached 2.4 per cent, giving investors a 7.08 per cent rate of return. As an investor, if you have a 10-15 per cent exposure to gold in your portfolio, you should start building it via gold exchange traded funds and sovereign gold bonds.

Before investing in gold, there are certain factors you need to understand about gold investment. If you decide to invest in the physical gold, there are extra costs in storing and insuring coins and bullion which can eat into your profit. It is preferable to invest in gold focused mutual funds and exchange traded funds, these can vastly reduce costs but also keep in mind that the price of gold is highly volatile. You should also discern whether your fund of choice aims to track the price of gold rather than gold mining companies.

2) Investors can beat inflation with I bonds.

I bond is a government issued security designed to beat inflation. I bonds help you preserve your money's purchasing power by making regular interest adjustments based on prevailing inflation. They charge investors interest rates every six months based on current inflation. Interest rates can change and can even go to zero.

This simply means that you may not necessarily lose your initial investment. But it still can be eaten away over time by inflation if interest rates fall. I bonds investment comes with lock in dates. This implies that you cannot cash out an I bond for at least a year after you buy it. And for the next four years, you will owe three months of interest as a penalty if you cash it out, more like a certificate of deposit.

3) Having a diversified portfolio is the best way to help you beat inflation as an investor

As an investor, how can you deal with high inflation? You need to reduce your expenses and save more. If your savings are not earning inflation returns, you might need to save a lot more to achieve your financial objectives. You should avoid investing in instruments that promise a higher rate of return. Smaller banks have higher interest rates than those offered by public and private sector banks. A good and balanced portfolio stands a good chance of providing inflation beating returns over the long term. You need to define your financial goals and then allocate to equities, debt and gold, depending on your investment horizon and risk tolerance.

4) Investors can beat inflation by investing in stocks

Investing in stocks is a good way to fend off inflation. From July

2012 to July 2022, U.S stocks have generated an average annualized return of nearly 11 per cent. After considering inflation, you will still look at about 8.3 per cent average annual returns. You should remember that investing in stocks is not risk free.

Investing in stocks is a good long term inflation hedge but you can also suffer in the short term if inflation spikes.

5) Investors can beat inflation by investing in cash.

Cash is usually overlooked as an inflation hedge during a surge. Cash is not a growth asset. It will keep up with inflation in nominal terms if inflation is accompanied by rising short term interest rates.

6) TIPS

TIPS is the abbreviation for Treasury Inflation-Protected Securities. Tips are quite easy to understand. They are government bonds that mirror the rise and fall of inflation. By this, when inflation goes up, the interest rate paid goes up too. Also, when deflation occurs, interest rates fall too. Adding TIPS to your portfolio can help balance your fixed income or bond portfolio since they're indexed to inflation. TIPS is considered one of the safest investments for your money and an effective way to diversify your investment because it is backed by the U.S federal government.

7) Investors can invest in real estate to beat inflation.

Real estate traditionally has been doing well during periods of higher inflation, and the value of properties can increase. This simply means that your landlord can increase your rent, which in turn increases their income so that it is on pace with the high inflation. Real estate investments can be made through real estate investment trusts (REITs) or through mutual funds that invest in REITs.

8) Investors can invest in commodities to beat inflation.

Raw materials like oil, metals and agricultural products always increase along with inflation. Investors need to know that commodities can also be extremely risky. The prices of goods depend mainly on supply and demand, supply and demand can be unpredictable. This makes it a very risky investment. Chances of rewards are high but the risk of losses is also high.

9) Investors can invest in cryptocurrency

Bitcoin is described as digital gold and it protects against inflation because of its limited supply. It is a good inflation hedge over the long term currently. Bitcoin is however very volatile, it can be difficult to incorporate into your diversified portfolio.

10) Leveraged loans

This is also a potential inflation hedge. Here, bankers and lenders can raise the interest rate charged so that the return on investment keeps up with the surging inflation. Investors do not necessarily own the debts themselves, rather, they invest in securities whose underlying assets are the loans.

Bottom line

- Various assets perform well during inflation
- Assets like real estate, commodities and certain types of bonds and stocks have historically been known to be good inflation hedges
- Inflation sensitive investments can be accessed in a variety of ways as either direct or indirect investments.
- Maintain a flexible budget that allows for temporary changes

- Structure your portfolio to include smart positions in asset classes that minimize the effects of an inflation surge
- Your efforts to eliminate the effects of inflation should not dominate the design of your financial portfolio, the strategies you employ should be able to complement your overall investment strategy.
- Be very careful with alternative assets
- Adjust your portfolio by shuffling your stocks and bonds
- Inflation is an opportunity for you to reexamine your portfolio
- Traditional inflation hedges do not always work

- There are zero guarantees.

The pros and cons of investing in inflation.

Every investment hedge has its pros and cons, just as every investment type has its pros and cons. It has been established that the main benefit of investing during inflation is to preserve the value of your portfolio. Another understandable reason is that you want to keep your investment growing.

Pros

- Preserve portfolio value
- To maintain income's buying power
- Diversify holdings

Cons

- Exposure to risks
- Diverts your long term goals
- Heavy portfolio in some classes.

How does Inflation affect asset values?

Inflation affects the economy and the value of assets can be unpredictable. Inflation damages the value of fixed rate debt securities because it Re values interest rate payments and also repayments of principal. If inflation rates surpass the interest rate, lenders are

affected. This is why it is
advisable for investors
to focus on real interest
rates sometimes.

CHAPTER 7

Conclusion

Investment can be a risky process until you realize that it is all about taking full control of your money in the long run. Investing requires learning, foresight, a responsible approach and patience. The kind of investment you decide to choose might likely depend on what you seek to gain in the long run and also the risks involved. Investments can be made in bonds, stocks, real estate, metals, money, assets, digital currencies and more.

Investors can choose to be independent without the help of an investment professional. Technology has also played a part by giving investors access to automated investment. The money needed to invest depends largely on the kind of investment and the financial position of the investor, also, as the needs and goals. Irrespective of how you choose to invest or what you choose to invest in, you need to research your target and your investment platform. Never invest in a business you have no idea about.